10-4-86

BROWN!

THE SPORTS CAREER OF JAMES BROWN

BY:

JAMES & LYNN HAHN

EDITED BY:

DR. HOWARD SCHROEDER

Professor in Reading and Language Arts
Dept. of Elementary Education
Mankato State University

CRESTWOOD HOUSE

Mankato, Minnesota

CIP

LIBRARY OF CONGRESS CATALOGING IN PUBLICATION DATA

Hahn, James.
 Brown! The sports career of James Brown.

 (Sports legends)
 SUMMARY: The football career of the famous running back at Syracuse University who played for nine seasons, from 1957 to 1965, with the Cleveland Browns.
 1. Brown, Jim, 1936-   — Juvenile literature. 2. Football players — United States — Biography — Juvenile literature. 3. Cleveland Browns (Football team: National League) — Juvenile literature. [1. Brown, Jim, 1936-
 . 2. Football players. 3. Afro-Americans — Biography] I. Hahn, Lynn. II. Schroeder, Howard. III. Title. IV. Series.
 GV939.B75H33   796.332'092'4   [B]   [92]   81-9837
 ISBN 0-89686-128-7 (lib. bdg.)   AACR2
 ISBN 0-89686-143-0 (pbk.)

INTERNATIONAL STANDARD BOOK NUMBERS:	LIBRARY OF CONGRESS CATALOG CARD NUMBER:
0-89686-128-7 Library Bound	81-9837
0-89686-143-0 Paperback	AACR2

PHOTO CREDITS:

Cover: Focus On Sports, Inc.

Wide World Photos: 3, 5, 15, 24-25, 30
Chamber of Commerce, St. Simons Island, GA: 6, 9
Manhassett High School: 12 (left and right), 13
Syracuse University: 17 (left)
United Press International: 17 (right), 18, 21, 22, 27,
          29, 32, 33, 41, 42-43, 44
Cleveland Browns: 38, 46

CRESTWOOD HOUSE

Crestwood House, Inc., Box 3427, Hwy. 66 So., Mankato, MN 56001

BROWN!

CHAPTER 1

In 1965, Jim Brown ran with a football for the last time. Fans haven't seen a better running back since then. Even the great O.J. Simpson couldn't break Jim Brown's running records.

Jim Brown played pro ball for just nine seasons (1957-1965). In that time he gained 12,312 yards for a 5.2 yard per carry average! He ran for a record-setting 106 touchdowns!

During his career he missed only one half of one game! Although injured many times, he didn't let the pain stop him from playing.

Jim Brown was born on February 17, 1936, on St. Simons Island. St. Simons Island is just off the mainland near the Georgia coastline in the Atlantic Ocean.

Theresa was Jim's mother's name and his father's name was Swinton. Jim's mother and father decided to live apart shortly after he was born. His mother went to New York to work and his father often traveled to find work. Nora Peterson, Jim's great-grandmother raised him. "To me, she was Mama," Jim said, "She was all I had, and I was all she had."

Jim's great-grandmother, although she was

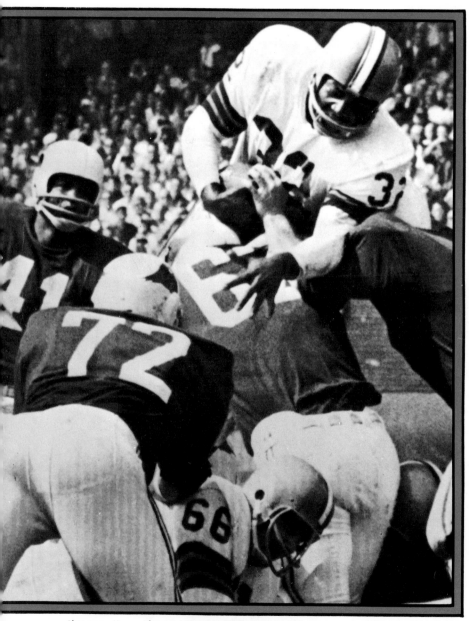

Jim goes "over the top" to score one of his 106 career touchdowns.

small, was tough. Sometimes Jim would stay out late, then sneak in through the back door. He'd tip-toe into his room, crawl into bed, and fall asleep.

Suddenly, he'd be awakened by the sting of a birch switch on his bottom. "That little old lady would stand there and whale the daylights out of me," Jim said.

Jim's great-grandmother also made sure he washed behind his ears and went to church every Sunday.

After church, Jim went out to play. His play-

Moss-hung trees on St. Simons Island.

grounds were different than most. "There were palm, fig, grapefruit, orange, and pecan trees," Jim said. "There were even a few banana trees. They were all fun to climb."

Jim also climbed moss-hung oak trees, cypress, cedar, longleaf pine, and magnolia trees. Sometimes Jim picked and ate the sweet wild grapes that grew on the trees.

When he got tired of climbing trees. Jim sat by the ocean. There, he watched porpoise roll in the surf. For fun, he counted the sandcrabs scurrying across the beach.

After resting by the beach, Jim ran down dirt roads into the dark woods. He explored murky marshlands and dove and swam in cool, clear ponds. On the bottoms of the ponds, Jim often found alligator bones.

Crabbing was Jim's favorite pastime. He'd sit on the edge of a pier and put a piece of meat in the middle of his crab basket. Then he'd drop the crab basket down to the ocean's floor.

Jim's crab basket was a square cage made with wire net. It had four gates, and each gate had a string tied to it. The four strings were tied to a longer string that Jim held. A jerk on the string would close the gates.

"I would sit there and try to guess whether Mr. Crab had come for supper," Jim said. "If I guessed right, I'd close the gates while he was inside eating."

If Jim was lucky, at the end of the day, he'd have a basket full of crabs. Then he'd boil them in water and eat the meat.

As a young boy, Jim wasn't bothered by the problems of black and white people. One day Jim saw a white boy fishing off a pier on St. Simons. "I stopped to talk with him," Jim said. "He had an extra rod and reel, and offered them to me. We fished there for a while and then went surf fishing."

"I played with white kids and black kids alike," Jim said. "We played together in Oglethorpe's Fort. That's where the British defeated the Spanish in the Battle of Bloody Marsh. We even dug for treasure that was supposed to have been buried by pirates."

Young Jim didn't play midget football or little league. There weren't any football fields, baseball diamonds, or basketball courts on St. Simons. However, Jim and his friends invented games. They used a piece of wood and a ball to play a stick-ball game, and they carved slingshots and made bows and arrows. Once, they even made a row boat.

Although Jim didn't play football as a young boy, he knew about the game. His father had been a semi-pro player in Georgia. Whenever his father was home, they talked football.

"I suppose I was born to be a fullback," Jim recalled years later. "Even as a little guy I was rough and tough. Some kids on St. Simons thought I was a little crazy. I'd fight with anybody, no matter how much older and bigger the other person was. It wasn't that I was mean; I just like rough contact."

When Jim was eight years old, his mother asked him to join her in New York. She had a job doing housework for a family. Before Jim left, his father gave him some advice. "Treat your mother

Jim and his friends had many hours of fun playing at Oglethorpe's Fort.

well," he said. "You may not always like what she tells you to do, but she's telling you for your own good."

CHAPTER 2

In New York Jim went to Plandome Road School in Manhasset. On his first day in school, he got into trouble. His mother had dressed him in a starched shirt and creased pants. She brushed his hair neatly and sent him to school in a cab.

"You look pretty, Sis," a boy said to Jim during recess.

"Well, good," Jim said, "Manhasset is going to be just as much fun as St. Simons Island." Then he knocked the boy down, jumped on him, and began punching him.

Jay Stranahan, the basketball and football coach at the school, told Jim to try sports instead of fighting. "Jimmy, you have many skills," he said. "Don't waste them."

Jim listened to the coach and began playing sports. The first football games he played in were on a corner lot. Before games, Jim and his friends had to clean the lot of rocks and broken glass.

As a teenager, Jim became a member of a gang. He was even elected warlord. "I never quite fit the image of a gang warlord," he said. "Though I never minded a fight, I never picked one. I didn't like bullies. The guys in the gang teased me for not smoking or drinking liquor. I couldn't see how either drinking or smoking would make me tougher."

Jim spent most of his time planning dances and parties for the gang. He also ordered fancy jackets for each gang member. The jackets were black and orchid colored. "We had our gang name lettered on the back and our names in front," Jim said. "The jackets were a big deal."

As a high school freshman, Jim had some problems. "I had no interest in studies," he said. However, many teachers tried to help him. Mrs. Virginia Hansen, a speech teacher, told him to make two and three-minute speeches. With her help, Jim became more skillful as a public speaker.

Ed Walsh, Manhasset High's football coach, also worked with Jim. "He was more than a great teacher of football," Jim said. "He was a builder of character. He cared about his kids, and would reach down into his own pocket to buy a needy student some clothing."

Although Jim was a first string halfback as a freshman, Coach Walsh wouldn't let him loaf. "If you want to take it easy, get off the first team," Coach Walsh yelled at Jim one day. "Get over there and play defense with the second team."

Jim did as the coach suggested. "I went over to

Football Coach, Ed Walsh (left photo) was one of Jim's best friends. Jim also played basketball well at Manhasset High.

the defense and did all I could to tear the first team apart," Jim said. "The next day I was back on the first team."

Coach Walsh told Jim to think about a sports career. "You can be a pro football player," he told Jim. "But, you've got to go to college first. You can't go to college unless you start studying."

Jim began studying hard and his grades improved.

As a sophomore football player, Jim averaged over seven yards per carry. Although he made the game look easy, Jim worked hard to develop his football skills.

"I've seen him eat a quick lunch, then run out on the field and work alone for the rest of the hour,"

Coach Walsh said. "When he wanted to learn something, he'd work after school and again in the evening. Sometimes I got phone calls from his mother. She asked if I could get him to come home and do his homework."

Once, during his junior year, Jim missed practice for five days. Coach Walsh telephoned him and asked why.

"I just didn't have any food, coach," Jim said. "I only had one piece of cake in five days. Mr. Walsh, you just don't know what it feels like to go through school and practice with no food!"

Jim (33) goes out for a pass in a 1952 Manhasset game.

Coach Walsh made sure Jim had enough food after that. Despite that problem, Jim had a great football season. He scored fourteen touchdowns and averaged fifteen yards per carry that year.

Racial prejudice was another problem Jim had to solve. "I used to hear what some players yelled at him," Coach Walsh said. "I heard mean things. But Jim never lost his head. He'd always tell me, 'Don't worry, Mr. Walsh, don't worry. I won't get angry.'"

As a senior, Jim scored twenty touchdowns and averaged 14.9 yards per carry. "It's hard to believe," Jim said years later, "but, I made better moves and cuts in high school than I made in college and pro ball."

Baseball, track, lacrosse, and basketball also interested Jim while in high school. In one basketball game he scored fifty-five points! As a senior, he averaged thirty-eight points per game.

Many colleges wanted Jim to play on their teams. Finally, he chose to play for Syracuse. However, he had to solve some problems there.

"At first, the Syracuse coaching staff had no interest in me," Jim said. "Some people thought a black man on the team only meant trouble."

"I would have worked as hard as any man on the squad. But, I didn't like being a black sheep. I became lazy. I started only one freshman game and played poorly."

Most of the students treated Jim as an equal.

Jim talks with his fellow students, Chuck Mayer (left) and Phyllis Goldstein.

"They did not regard me as a Black Menance," he said. "They were friendly and completely natural with me."

Although he got along with his teammates, Jim felt discouraged. Since he had been a football star in high school, he had expected to play first string in college.

After his freshman football season, Jim wanted to leave Syracuse. He told a friend he planned to quit school.

"It's too soon to quit," the friend advised Jim. "Stick it out, study hard, and keep up your grades. If they give you a bad deal next year, then quit."

Jim decided to stick it out. However, the coaches surprised him at the start of his sophomore year. They dropped him even lower to fifth string halfback!

"Well, that's all right," Jim said. "I'll just go out and hustle."

Each day after practice, the team had to run three laps around the football field. That was almost one mile. Instead of jogging the laps like most of the others, Jim ran them. "Running those laps almost killed me," Jim said. "But, I always finished first or second."

After running the laps, Jim looked at the coaches. "I could see the coaches thinking," Jim said. "Maybe Brown is ready to play some football." In a short time, the coaches moved Jim up to second string.

Then, Jim got his big chance! In a game against Villanova, the coaches sent him in. "On the very first play of my college career," Jim said, "I fumbled! I wasn't even hit. I just dropped the ball!"

The coaches took Jim out of the game right away.

Despite that failure, Jim didn't give up. Instead, he worked harder in practice. The coaches saw this and let Jim play in a game against Cornell.

On one play, Jim ran fifty-four yards for a touchdown! "I gained 151 yards in that game and won a first-string job at last," he said. "This was the turning point of my career. Up until that time, I'd just been another player. But, from that game on I was first string!"

Jim hustled and stuck with it, and it paid off. "If you work hard and have the right attitude," Jim said, "things will work out for the best. When things don't go smoothly, just lay in there and something will break."

Jim made the first string when he was only a sophomore at Syracuse.

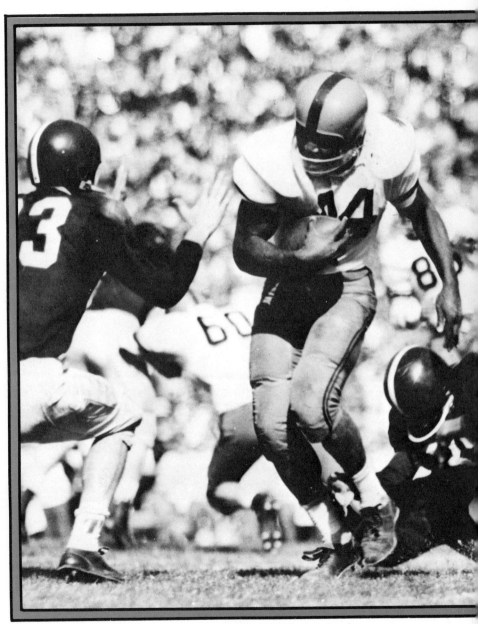

Jim is about to be tackled after a long gain in the 1957 Cotton Bowl.

As a junior, Jim had to solve more problems. "I became a goof-off," he said. "I forgot that being a sports star doesn't excuse a man from being something as a person. I studied only hard enough to get C's."

Before it was too late, Jim decided to work harder. "I began earning C+'s and B-'s," he said. "Logic became my favorite course. I learned many important things that shaped my life. The most important thing I learned was nothing is all black or all white. When a man loses sight of this, he can't tell right from wrong."

On the football field, Jim had a great year. He was one of the best runners among the colleges in the East.

As a senior, Jim set a national record in a game against Colgate. He ran for 197 yards and scored 43 points!

In the 1957 Cotton Bowl, Jim scored twenty-one points and was named the game's best player!

At Syracuse, Jim also starred in lacrosse and track and field.

In four years, Jim had learned a lot about football and life. "I learned there is no substitute for hard work," he said. "Once, I had been as far down as an athlete can be. But, I had come from nothing to something. I knew that having to fight my way up was the best thing for me."

CHAPTER 3

The Cleveland Browns liked the way Jim ran with the football. After many days of contract talk, Jim and the Browns agreed to a $15,000 per year contract.

To celebrate, Jim bought a new car. "It was a convertible," he said. "It was bright red with a white top and white trim. It was the biggest and best car that a down payment could buy."

However, before he could play with the Browns, Jim had to solve other problems. "I wanted a nice apartment near our practice field," he said. "I wanted to live in a nice neighborhood. But, I had a hard time finding a place to live."

"We only take whites," one landlady told Jim.

Finally, Jim found housing he was happy with. Then, he could concentrate on learning to play pro football. "My biggest running fault," he said "was hitting the line with my head down and my eyes closed."

Soon, Jim learned how to keep his eyes open. Then, few players could stop him. "I saw three men trying to tackle him," said one defensive player. "But Jim ran right through them."

In 1957, Jim's rookie year, he helped Cleveland

win the Eastern Conference title. He scored ten touchdowns and led the league in rushing with 942 yards. "I felt that I had earned my fifteen thousand dollars," he said after the season.

"What kind of man is Jim Brown off the field?" sportswriters asked his teammates.

Jim was happy to learn that he led the balloting for the NFL All-Star team. He was the first rookie to top the list.

For his 1957 performance, Jim was given the Marlboro Rookie-of-the-Year
award.

"Jim is a quiet fellow," said one teammate.

"He seldom starts talking until someone asks him a question," said another teammate. "He thinks before he speaks."

"Jim is a cool human being off the field," said another. "He doesn't complain and doesn't bother people."

Writers asked defensive players what kind of football player Jim was. "He's superman," one player said. "You can forget Bronco Nagurski and Jim Thorpe. I'll take Jim Brown!"

During Jim's rookie year, some players hit him very hard. "Why don't you yell at players who treat you roughly?" a writer asked Jim.

"I refuse to argue with players," Jim said. "That's not my style. I react to every tackle the same way. When a guy hits me hard enough to rattle my bones, I get up without saying a thing. I walk back to the huddle without expression. When he hits me a little less hard, I do the same thing. That way, my opponent never knows if he's getting under my skin. After a while I may begin to get under his skin."

After his rookie season, Jim had to spend some time in the Army. He was stationed at Fort Benning, Georgia.

When Jim reported to football training camp the next year he had lost eight pounds. Writers asked him why.

Jim hurdles through a big hole to score a 1958 touchdown.

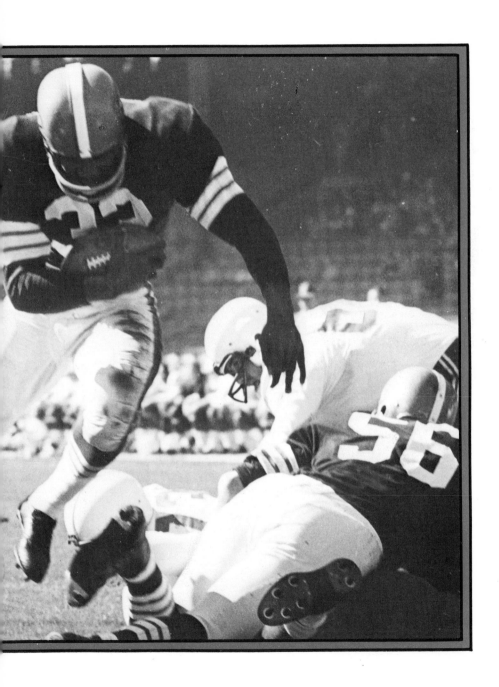

"Army lieutenants don't eat well," Jim laughed.

1958 was a very good year for Jim. He gained 1,527 yards, setting a National Football League (NFL) rushing record! He scored eighteen touchdowns, tying a record. Every time he carried the ball, he averaged 5.9 yards!

For this great season, Jim was awarded the Jim Thorpe Trophy as the Most Valuable Player.

Although Jim had a great season, the Cleveland Browns didn't. They lost the Eastern Division play-off to the New York Giants, 10-0.

At press conferences after games, writers asked players how to stop Jim.

"I don't know how to tackle him," one player said. "I haven't been able to catch up to him yet."

"Tackle him above the waist and holler for help," another player said. "If you don't, he'll drag you to death."

"All I do is grab hold, hang on, and wait for help," said another.

"He's the only player I know who can run faster sideways than straight ahead," said one player. "If you do hit him," said another player, "he runs right out of your arms."

"I had one of my best days against Jim Brown," said one player. "I made almost as much yardage as he did — riding on his back!"

"The only way I've found to stop him is to hit him right at the ankles with your shoulder," said a

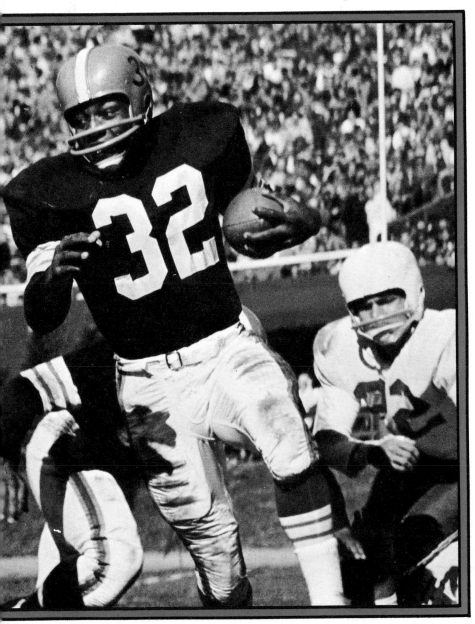

Jim heads upfield after breaking through the line.

player. "Otherwise, it's like tackling a train!"

Jim's teammates helped him gain yards by blocking for him. "I'd like to give credit to the linemen who opened holes for me," Jim said. "The fact is, I never would've been able to run without linemen clearing a path for me. The line and I work well together. That's the important thing."

Another reason Jim ran so well was he stayed in shape. "I don't smoke," he said, "nor do I drink."

Shopping for clothes was one way Jim relaxed. "I like to dress neatly," he said. He had fun buying and wearing expensive suits and silk shirts. "Jim has shoes on top of shoes, hats on top of hats, and suits on top of suits," said a friend.

Except for his expensive clothes, Jim lived like most people. "You'd never know he was a big star," said a neighbor. "In the spring we talk about how to get the grass to grow better."

A generous man, Jim bought his wife fur coats, perfumes, and jewelry. His children had more toys than they could play with.

CHAPTER 4

Before the 1959 season, Jim signed a new contract. The Cleveland Browns were now paying him

Diving past the goal post, Jim scores in a 1959 game against San Francisco.

$25,000 to play football.

"How do you get ready for a game?" writers asked Jim one afternoon.

"On the Saturday before a game I'll eat dinner with the team," Jim said. "Then we'll all go to a movie. After that I think hard about what I've got to do. Finally, I get a good night's sleep."

During the 1959 season, defensive players tackled Jim hard. In one game, he got a hit he'll never forget. "On our first play I ran off tackle and got swarmed over," he said. "In the pileup someone kicked me in the head and I suffered a loss

In a 1960 game, Jim tries to go around the left side of the New York Giants' line. He gained three yards.

of memory. I stayed in the game, but couldn't remember my assignments. I couldn't even remember having come into the stadium for the game. Our quarterback had to explain my assignments to me in the huddle. I carried the ball by instinct." However, Jim recovered and rushed for 1,329 yards that season!

After the football season, Jim got a job in the marketing department of a soft drink company. "I was not hired just for publicity," Jim said. "It wasn't a part-time job, either. I was on salary and on call throughout the year."

In 1960, Jim signed another contract with the Cleveland Browns for $32,000 per year. Although he played with a badly bruised ankle most of the year, Jim still gained 1,257 yards! Jim wasn't happy though, because the Cleveland Browns finished in second place.

To relax after games, Jim stayed home with his wife and children or went to movies. "I especially enjoy foreign movies," he said. "It takes hours to let my body settle down. I can't go out and party like some of the guys."

"What's a typical day for you?" writers asked Jim.

"I get up at 8:30 in the morning," Jim said. "For breakfast I'll have four pancakes, sausage, and orange juice. I don't eat very much. Then I have to be at practice at 9:30."

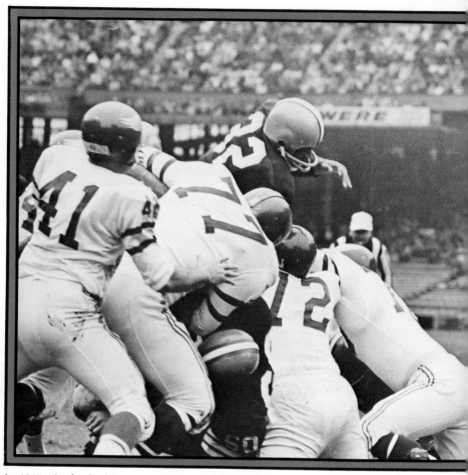

In 1961, Jim broke his own rushing mark for a single game, by gaining 242 yards in a game against the Eagles. However, on this play he was stopped.

"After practice everyday I'll listen to some records. I enjoy jazz, rhythm and blues, and dance tunes. I don't like classical records."

"On Saturdays, I sleep until noon. After I eat, I answer my fan letters. Next, I read some newspa-

Jim spends some time with his son, Kevin, in this 1961 photo.

pers and magazines. After that, I study football plays."

1961 was a super year for Jim Brown. He gained 1,408 yards running. "It's been a long season," he later told writers. "I'm just glad I was able to come through without injury."

Although Jim played well, the Browns didn't. The team finished in third place.

In 1962, Jim was earning $45,000. However, that year proved to be one of his hardest. In a game against Dallas, a defender smashed Jim's left wrist. A

Jim follows his blockers upfield.

trainer taped it and Jim continued to play. Although it was swollen and painful for many games, he still played.

Then Jim played a poor game against Washington. "The Redskins game was the most miserable of my career," he recalled. "I made two horrible mistakes. In the first quarter I slanted off left tackle, but couldn't find anywhere to run. So I tossed a lateral to a teammate. One of the Redskins picked it off and ran it back thirty-nine yards for a touchdown. In the fourth quarter, I fumbled and the Redskins recovered."

Things didn't improve for Jim as the season went on. In a game against the New York Giants, defenders hit him hard. "They hit my eyes with forearms and elbows," he said. "At least seven times they dug through my face bar."

"At the end of each game, Jim is the sorest player in the dressing room," said a teammate. "They really give him a going over."

Despite his problems, Jim still had faith in God. "I think you need a little help from Upstairs," he said. "You need someone looking out for you. You can't control everything."

The Cleveland Browns finished third in 1962 and Jim Brown was second in rushing with just 996 yards. That was the first time he failed to reach the one thousand yard mark.

"Though most people never knew it," Jim said,

"I played part of the year with a badly sprained wrist. It was tough for me to hold the ball. I couldn't shift it from hand to hand in the open field."

Jim had another problem that season. He didn't get along with Paul Brown, head coach of the Cleveland Browns. "Once I walked into a squad meeting five minutes late," Jim said. "I was in a restaurant and the clock was running slow."

"That'll cost you fifty dollars," Coach Brown said as Jim took his seat.

Jim also didn't like the plays Coach Brown called. He and some other players talked the Browns' owners into hiring a new coach.

CHAPTER 5

In 1963, Jim played for Blanton Collier, the new head coach. However, a new coach couldn't make the defenders take it easy on Jim. In one game a defender clubbed Jim in the eye with a forearm. "I slugged him back," Jim said, "and he came back swinging. The refs kicked both of us out of the game! Anyone is welcome to try anything to tackle me. But, nobody's going to endanger my eyesight without getting a fight."

Jim had to solve more physical problems that

Jim leaves defenders lying in the dust, as he breaks through the line.

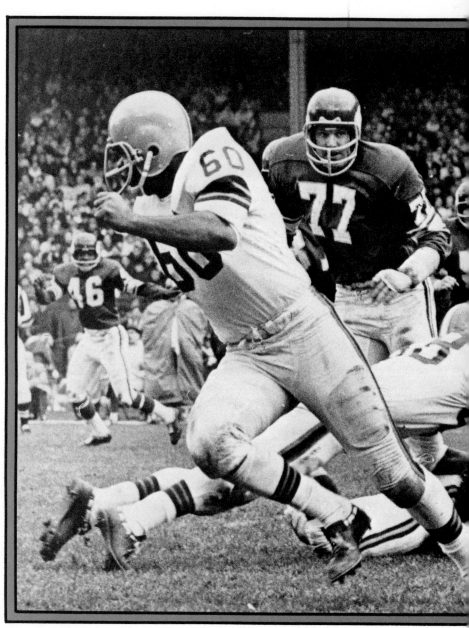

With a smile on his face, Jim turns on the steam in a game against the Minnesota Vikings.

38

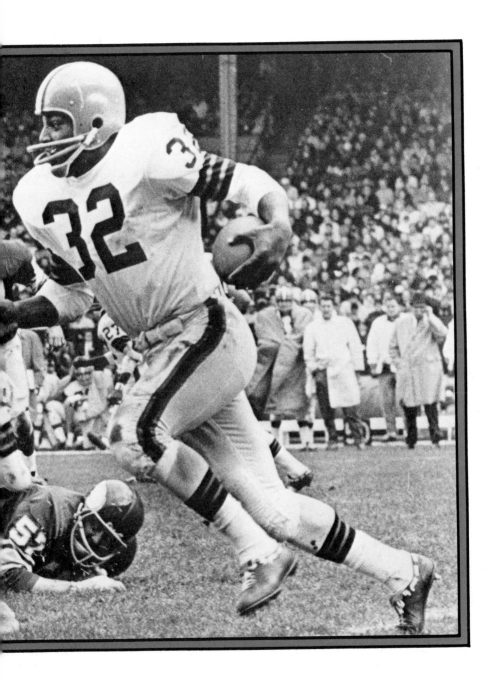

year. "I had water on the elbow that hurt with every contact," he said. "After a game my arm was so swollen I had trouble putting on a shirt."

Despite the pain, Jim had a great year. He scored touchdowns on 80, 71, 59, and 62-yard runs. For the season, he gained 1,863 yards, a new NFL record! The players voted him the most valuable player in the league.

"How do you do it?" writers asked Jim.

"As I take the ball from the quarterback, I watch my block develop," Jim said. "Then I decide on just how fast to go. I stay with my blocker. When he starts to make contact, I shoot by him. Most of the time I'll hit a big pileup. Because there are a lot of guys around, the defense thinks they have me. I never feel I'm caught until I'm down!"

Although Jim was a great runner, his teammates were more important to him than gaining yards. He said many times he'd rather win games than gain yards.

"Jim is our team's source of inspiration," said a teammate. "He cares about the defense and their problems. He thanks the line for their good blocks."

"Jim taught me to strive for perfection in practice," another said. "This makes you play better in games. After practice he'll do extra running. He doesn't need it for himself because he's always in shape. He's setting a model for his teammates."

"He's sincere, eager, and tough," said a coach.

Several New York Giants tried to stop him, but Jim scored the first of three touchdowns he got in this 1963 game.

"He never even takes a sip of water during a game. After a game he'll have a soft drink."

1964 was a great year for the Cleveland Browns and Jim Brown. On December 27th, Jim carried the ball 27 times and gained 114 yards. His running helped his teammates beat the Baltimore Colts 27-0

Jim gains important yardage in the 1964 title game against the Colts.

to win the NFL title!

Although a hurt toe bothered Jim throughout the year, he was still able to gain 1,446 yards.

After the football season, Jim spoke out boldly for the rights of black people. He gave $50,000 of his own money to start a black business program in

Jim and his wife, Sue, attend the premiere of The Dirty Dozen, a 1967 film in which Jim was featured.

Cleveland. He helped blacks start small businesses near where they lived. "Get off the streets," Jim told black people in his speeches. "Get into the schools, the colleges, and the libraries. Become well educated."

The 1965 football season was another great one for Jim. He ran for 1,544 yards and scored twenty-one touchdowns! He won the Jim Thorpe trophy again.

With Jim's help, the Cleveland Browns won the Eastern Division Crown. However, the Green Bay Packers beat them for the NFL championship.

In July, 1966, Jim surprised the sports world. He said he was retiring from football. "I quit with regret, but no sorrow," he said. "You should get out while you're on top. I've been able to do all I wanted in football. Football was fun! If I hadn't been good enough to make the pros, I would have played sandlot ball."

To earn a living, Jim decided to be an actor. Although acting looks like an easy job, it isn't. As an actor, Jim was beaten by bandits, dragged by horses, and even trapped in a flaming house! "I feel like I played four quarters with a football team on my back," Jim said after making one film.

Jim's acting skills impressed other actors. "He looks good, and speaks and thinks well, too," said one actor.

As an actor, Jim had one goal — to please his

fans. "I want people to look at me and say they had fun," he said.

"My beliefs are simple," Jim said many times. "I believe in a Supreme Power and in treating my neighbors right. I am a Baptist, but I don't believe other religions are wrong."

It's been quite some time since Jim Brown played football. Yet, many of his records still stand. Whenever a rookie runs well, people compare him to Jim Brown. Someday, someone may break Jim's records. However, thousands of fans will never forget the way Jim Brown ran with the ball.

AFTERWORD

Jim Brown is currently living in Hollywood, California. He works as an actor and sports announcer. Since boxing interests Jim, he sometimes promotes and announces boxing matches. Jim also advises young black people about business and personal problems when he has free time.

IF YOU ENJOYED THIS STORY, THERE ARE MORE LEGENDS TO READ ABOUT: